SMOOTHIES FOR ARTHRITIS

Quick and Easy Delicious Arthritis Friendly Smoothie Recipes to Relief Arthritis, Muscle pain and Inflammation

STEVE K. PARKINS

Copyright © 2023 Steve K. Parkins

All rights reserved. No part of this publication may be reproduced, distributed, or transmitted in any form or by any means, including photocopying, recording, or other electronic or mechanical methods, without the prior written permission of the publisher, except in the case of brief quotations embodied in critical reviews and certain other noncommercial uses permitted by copyright law.

YOU CAN ALSO CHECK RELATED BOOK

JUICING FOR ARTHRITIS

TABLE OF CONTENTS

INTRODUCTION 5
DELICIOUS SMOOTHIES FOR ARTHRITIS 8
   1. Smoothie with tropical turmeric 8
   2. Smoothie Berry Blast 8
   3. Green Goddess Smoothie 9
   4. Cherry-Almond Smoothie 9
   5. Ginger Pineapple Smoothie 10
   6. Smoothie with orange creamsicle 10
   7. Mango and turmeric smoothie 11
   8. Avocado and Blueberry Smoothie 11
   9. Blended Papaya with Mint 12
   10. Smoothie with spinach and flaxseed 12
   11. Mango-turmeric smoothie 13
   12. Raspberry-Beet Smoothie 14
   13. Smoothie with green tea and berries 14
   14. Ginger-carrot smoothie 15
   15. Smoothie with pineapple and cucumber 15
   16. Smoothie with spinach and berries 16
   17. Smoothie with watermelon and mint 16
   18. Ginger-Peach Smoothie 17
   19. A mango-papaya smoothie 18
   20. Lemon-Kiwi Smoothie 18
   21. Smoothie with orange, carrot, and turmeric 19

22. Flaxseed and Strawberry Smoothie 19
23. Smoothie with kale, pineapple, and coconut 20
24. Cherry-Almond Smoothie... 21
25. Avocado and Blueberry Smoothie 21
26. A mango coconut chia smoothie.............................. 22
27. Green Smoothie with Pineapples, Mint 23
28. Smoothie with raspberries and nuts 23
29. Smoothie with apple cinnamon................................ 24
30. Mango Ginger Turmeric Smoothie.......................... 25
31. Cherry-Almond Smoothie... 25
32. Avocado and Blueberry Smoothie 26
33. A mango coconut chia smoothie.............................. 27
34. Green Smoothie with Pineapples, Mint 27
35. Smoothie with raspberries and nuts 28
36. Smoothie with apple cinnamon................................ 29
37. Mango Ginger Turmeric Smoothie.......................... 29
38. Shake with blueberries and flaxseed....................... 30
39. Smoothie with mango and turmeric 31
40. Smoothie with Kale, Ginger, Pineapple................... 31
41. Coconut and Papaya Smoothie 32
42. Smoothie with almonds and spinach....................... 33
43. Strawberry Chia Smoothie....................................... 34
44. Smoothie with pineapple, mint, and lime 34
45. Smoothie with Peach, Ginger, and Turmeric........... 35
CONCLUSION.. 36

INTRODUCTION

In a small town Sarah was a woman who lived among undulating hills. She had been battling with arthritis for years, enduring the persistent pain and stiffness that had become a part of her daily life. Sarah had tried numerous treatments and medications, desperately seeking relief from the debilitating symptoms that limited her mobility and joy.

One fateful day, while browsing through a local health fair, Sarah stumbled upon a booth dedicated to holistic approaches for managing arthritis. She started a discussion with him out of curiosity. a passionate nutritionist named Emma, who shared her own personal journey of healing through nutrition.

Empowered by Emma's story and armed with newfound hope, Sarah delved into extensive research and discovered the profound impact that food could have on managing arthritis. She embarked on a mission to create a collection of smoothie recipes that would not only be delicious but also provide targeted nourishment for her aching joints.

Guided by her newfound knowledge, Sarah carefully selected a variety of anti-inflammatory fruits, nutrient-rich vegetables, and healing spices to incorporate into her smoothie recipes. Each concoction was thoughtfully crafted to deliver a strong mixture of vitamins, minerals, and antioxidants, with the sole purpose of alleviating inflammation and promoting joint health.

As Sarah faithfully sipped on these vibrant elixirs, she began to notice remarkable changes within her body. The pain and stiffness gradually subsided, and she regained a sense of freedom she thought she had lost forever. Energized and determined, Sarah shared her recipes and experiences with friends and family, witnessing their own transformative journeys towards arthritis relief.

Word of Sarah's incredible success quickly spread, reaching countless individuals seeking alternative solutions for managing their arthritis symptoms. Her passion for helping others inspired her to compile her collection of recipes into a comprehensive guidebook, the Tasty Arthritis Smoothie Cookbook.

Within the pages of this cookbook, readers are introduced to a wide array of flavorful and nutritious smoothie recipes designed to nourish the body, reduce inflammation, and support joint health. Each recipe is accompanied by detailed instructions and a list of carefully selected Ingredients, ensuring that anyone can easily recreate these healing in the convenience of their kitchen. The Tasty Arthritis Smoothie Cookbook is an invaluable tool to help you take charge of your health and start on a path to improved wellbeing, regardless of how long you've had arthritis or if you just got a new diagnosis. It is a testament to the impact of diet in finding relief and regaining a life filled with vitality.

Are you ready to embark on your own journey towards arthritis relief? Grab your copy of the Tasty Arthritis Smoothie Cookbook and discover a world of delicious, healing recipes that will revitalize your body and rejuvenate your spirit. Let the impact of diet guide you on the path to renewed wellness and a life free from the constraints of arthritis.

DELICIOUS SMOOTHIES FOR ARTHRITIS

1. Smoothie with tropical turmeric

Ingredients

1 cup pineapple chunks,

1 banana,

1 tsp turmeric powder,

1 cup coconut milk,

Small amount of spinach.

Preparation

Blend till creamy and smooth.

Pour into a glass, then sip.

2. Smoothie Berry Blast

Ingredients

Mixed Berries ((strawberries, blueberries, raspberries) 1 Cup

Almond milk, 1 cup

1 tbsp of chia seeds

1 scoop of collagen powder

Preparation

All the Ingredients should be blended together

Serve and Enjoy

3. Green Goddess Smoothie

Ingredients

Spinach, 1 cup,

1 pear,

1/2 avocados,

1 teaspoon fresh ginger,

1 cup coconut water,

1 cup freshly squeezed lemon

Preparation

Blend all of the Ingredients in a blender to make it. Blend until smooth and creamy. Pour into a glass to serve.

4. Cherry-Almond Smoothie

Ingredients

Frozen cherries, 1 cup

Almond milk, 1 cup,

1 teaspoon almond butter,

Pinch of cinnamon

Preparation

Should all be blended together to make the dish. Blend until smooth and creamy. Sip after pouring into a glass.

5. Ginger Pineapple Smoothie

Ingredients

1 cup of fresh pineapple slices,

1 tiny piece of ginger root,

1 cup of coconut water,

Small amount of kale.

Preparation

Blend everything well and easily. Pour into a glass to serve.

6. Smoothie with orange creamsicle

Ingredients

one banana, frozen

Peeled and segmented orange, one

almond milk, 1 cup Vanilla essence squirt

Preparation

Prepare by blending all the Ingredients in a blender. Blend until smooth and creamy. Sip after pouring into a glass.

7. Mango and turmeric smoothie

Ingredients

1 cup frozen mango pieces,

1 teaspoon turmeric powder,

1 cup coconut milk,

little amount of baby spinach.

Preparation

Combine all the Ingredients in a blender and blend until smooth. Everything should be completely blended until smooth.

8. Avocado and Blueberry Smoothie

Ingredients

Blueberries, 1 cup

12 an avocado

almond milk, 1 cup

10 grams of hemp seeds

Preparation

In a blender, combine all the Ingredients.

Blend till creamy and smooth.

To serve, pour into a glass.

9. Blended Papaya with Mint

Ingredients

1 cup of chunks of fresh papaya

a few leaves of fresh mint

Coconut water, 1 cup

lime squeeze

Preparation

Blend the items together in a blender.

Blend everything thoroughly until it's smooth.

Pour into a glass, then sip.

10. Smoothie with spinach and flaxseed

Ingredients

spinach, 1 cup

1-tablespoon flaxseed meal

almond milk, 1 cup

1-tablespoon almond butter

1 teaspoon of honey

Preparation

To a blender, add all the Ingredients.

Blend till creamy and smooth.

To serve, pour into a glass.

11. *Mango-turmeric smoothie*

Ingredients

1 cup of chunks of frozen mango

1-tablespoon turmeric powder

almond milk, 1 cup

1 tablespoon of honey

Preparation

In a blender, combine all the Ingredients.

Blend till creamy and smooth.

Pour into a glass, then sip.

12. Raspberry-Beet Smoothie

Ingredients

raspberries, 1 cup

1 small, cooked, and peeled beet

Coconut water, 1 cup

a tbsp of chia seeds

Preparation

To a blender, add all the Ingredients.

Blend everything thoroughly and smoothly.

To serve, pour into a glass.

13. Smoothie with green tea and berries

Ingredients

Blueberries, 1 cup

1 cup chilled, brewed green tea

one banana

little amount of baby spinach

Preparation

Blend the items together in a blender.

Blend till creamy and smooth.

Pour into a glass, then sip.

14. Ginger-carrot smoothie

Ingredients

1 large, peeled, and sliced carrot

1 miniature ginger root

almond milk, 1 cup

1 tablespoon of honey

Preparation

In a blender, combine all the Ingredients.

Blend everything thoroughly until it's smooth.

To serve, pour into a glass.

15. Smoothie with pineapple and cucumber

Ingredients

1 cup of chunks of fresh pineapple

half a cucumber

Coconut water, 1 cup

lime squeeze

Preparation

To a blender, add all the Ingredients.

Blend till creamy and smooth.

Serve in a glass, then sip.

16. Smoothie with spinach and berries

Ingredients

Strawberry, blueberry, and raspberry-filled 1 cup of mixed berries

spinach, 1 cup

almond milk, 1 cup

1-tablespoon flaxseed meal

Preparation

Blend the items together in a blender.

Blend everything thoroughly until it's smooth.

To serve, pour into a glass.

17. Smoothie with watermelon and mint

Ingredients

2 cups pieces of fresh watermelon

a few leaves of fresh mint

Coconut water, 1 cup

lemon squeeze

Preparation

In a blender, combine all the Ingredients.

Blend till creamy and smooth.

Pour into a glass, then sip.

18. Ginger-Peach Smoothie

Ingredients

1 pitted and sliced ripe peach

1 miniature ginger root

almond milk, 1 cup

1 teaspoon of honey

Preparation

To a blender, add all the Ingredients.

Blend everything thoroughly until it's smooth.

Serve in a glass, then sip.

19. A mango-papaya smoothie

Ingredients

1 cup of chunks of frozen mango

1 cup of chunks of fresh papaya

Coconut water, 1 cup

a tbsp of chia seeds

Preparation

Blend the items together in a blender.

Blend till creamy and smooth.

To serve, pour into a glass.

20. Lemon-Kiwi Smoothie

Ingredients

sliced and peeled two ripe kiwis

1 lime's juice

almond milk, 1 cup

1 tablespoon of honey

Preparation

In a blender, combine all the Ingredients.

Blend everything thoroughly until it's smooth.

Pour into a glass, then sip.

21. Smoothie with orange, carrot, and turmeric

Ingredients

1 large, peeled, and sliced carrot

Peeled and segmented orange, one

fresh turmeric root, peeled, 1/2 inch

almond milk, 1 cup

1 tablespoon of honey

Preparation

Blend the items together in a blender.

Blend till creamy and smooth.

To serve, pour into a glass.

22. Flaxseed and Strawberry Smoothie

Ingredients

1 cup of strawberries, frozen

one ripe banana

almond milk, 1 cup

1-tablespoon flaxseed meal

1 teaspoon of honey

Preparation

To a blender, add all the Ingredients.

Blend everything thoroughly until it's smooth.

Pour into a glass, then sip.

23. Smoothie with kale, pineapple, and coconut

Ingredients

1 cup of kale leaves, chopped

1 cup of chunky pineapple

50 ml of coconut milk

50 ml of coconut water

lime squeeze

Preparation

In a blender, combine all the Ingredients.

Blend till creamy and smooth.

To serve, pour into a glass.

24. Cherry-Almond Smoothie

Ingredients

Frozen cherries, 1 cup

50 ml of almond milk

Greek yogurt, half a cup

1-tablespoon almond butter

1 teaspoon of honey

Preparation

Blend the items together in a blender.

Blend everything thoroughly until it's smooth.

Serve in a glass, then sip.

25. Avocado and Blueberry Smoothie

Ingredients

Blueberries, 1 cup

ripe avocado, half

almond milk, 1 cup

1 tablespoon of honey

Preparation

To a blender, add all the Ingredients.

Blend till creamy and smooth.

To serve, pour into a glass.

26. A mango coconut chia smoothie

Ingredients

1 cup of chunks of frozen mango

50 ml of coconut milk

50 ml of coconut water

a tbsp of chia seeds

1 teaspoon of honey

Preparation

In a blender, combine all the Ingredients.

Blend everything thoroughly until it's smooth.

Pour into a glass, then sip.

27. Green Smoothie with Pineapples, Mint

Ingredients

one cup of new spinach

1 cup of chunky pineapple

a few leaves of fresh mint

Coconut water, 1 cup

Preparation

Blend the items together in a blender.

Blend till creamy and smooth.

Serve in a glass, then sip.

28. Smoothie with raspberries and nuts

Ingredients

raspberries, 1 cup

walnuts, 1/4 cup

almond milk, 1 cup

1 teaspoon of honey

Preparation

To a blender, add all the Ingredients.

Blend everything thoroughly until it's smooth.

To serve, pour into a glass.

29. Smoothie with apple cinnamon

Ingredients

1 medium apple, cut after being peeled

Oats, rolled, in a cup

almond milk, 1 cup

1-tablespoon maple syrup

12 teaspoon cinnamon

Preparation

In a blender, combine all the Ingredients.

Blend everything thoroughly until it's smooth.

Pour into a glass, then sip.

30. Mango Ginger Turmeric Smoothie

Ingredients

1 cup of chunks of frozen mango

fresh turmeric root, peeled, 1/2 inch

fresh ginger root, peeled, 1/2 inch

Coconut water, 1 cup

1 teaspoon of honey

Preparation

Blend the items together in a blender.

Blend till creamy and smooth.

To serve, pour into a glass.

31. Cherry-Almond Smoothie

Ingredients

Frozen cherries, 1 cup

50 ml of almond milk

Greek yogurt, half a cup

1-tablespoon almond butter

1 teaspoon of honey

Preparation

Blend the items together in a blender.

Blend everything thoroughly until it's smooth.

Serve in a glass, then sip.

32. Avocado and Blueberry Smoothie

Ingredients

Blueberries, 1 cup

ripe avocado, half

almond milk, 1 cup

1 tablespoon of honey

Preparation

To a blender, add all the Ingredients.

Blend till creamy and smooth.

To serve, pour into a glass.

33. A mango coconut chia smoothie

Ingredients

1 cup of chunks of frozen mango

50 ml of coconut milk

50 ml of coconut water

a tbsp of chia seeds

1 teaspoon of honey

Preparation

In a blender, combine all the Ingredients.

Blend everything thoroughly until it's smooth.

Pour into a glass, then sip.

34. Green Smoothie with Pineapples, Mint

Ingredients

one cup of new spinach

1 cup of chunky pineapple

a few leaves of fresh mint

Coconut water, 1 cup

Preparation

Blend the items together in a blender.

Blend till creamy and smooth.

Serve in a glass, then sip.

35. Smoothie with raspberries and nuts

Ingredients

raspberries, 1 cup

walnuts, 1/4 cup

almond milk, 1 cup

1 teaspoon of honey

Preparation

To a blender, add all the Ingredients.

Blend everything thoroughly until it's smooth.

To serve, pour into a glass.

36. Smoothie with apple cinnamon

Ingredients

1 medium apple, cut after being peeled

Oats, rolled, in a cup

almond milk, 1 cup

1-tablespoon maple syrup

12 teaspoon cinnamon

Preparation

In a blender, combine all the Ingredients.

Blend everything thoroughly until it's smooth.

Pour into a glass, then sip.

37. Mango Ginger Turmeric Smoothie

Ingredients

1 cup of chunks of frozen mango

fresh turmeric root, peeled, 1/2 inch

fresh ginger root, peeled, 1/2 inch

Coconut water, 1 cup

1 teaspoon of honey

Preparation

Blend the items together in a blender.

Blend till creamy and smooth.

To serve, pour into a glass.

38. Shake with blueberries and flaxseed

Ingredients

Blueberries, 1 cup

one banana

Ground flaxseed, 1 tablespoon

almond milk, 1 cup

1 teaspoon of honey

Preparation

To a blender, add all the Ingredients.

Blend till creamy and smooth.

Pour into a glass, then sip.

39. Smoothie with mango and turmeric

Ingredients

1 cup of chunks of frozen mango

fresh turmeric root, peeled, 1/2 inch

fresh ginger root, peeled, 1/2 inch

Coconut water, 1 cup

1 teaspoon of honey

Preparation

Blend the items together in a blender.

Blend everything thoroughly until it's smooth.

Serve in a glass, then sip.

40. Smoothie with Kale, Ginger, Pineapple

Ingredients

1 cup of kale, chopped

1 cup of chunky pineapple

fresh ginger root, peeled, 1/2 inch

Coconut water, 1 cup

1 teaspoon of honey

Preparation

In a blender, combine all the Ingredients.

Blend till creamy and smooth.

To serve, pour into a glass.

41. Coconut and Papaya Smoothie

Ingredients

1 cup sliced ripe papaya

1 cup of chunks of frozen mango

50 ml of coconut milk

50 ml of coconut water

1 teaspoon of honey

Preparation

To a blender, add all the Ingredients.

Blend everything thoroughly until it's smooth.

Pour into a glass, then sip.

42. Smoothie with almonds and spinach

Ingredients

a few crisp spinach leaves

one banana

quarter cup of almond butter

almond milk, 1 cup

1 teaspoon of honey

Preparation

Blend the items together in a blender.

Blend till creamy and smooth.

Serve in a glass, then sip.

43. Strawberry Chia Smoothie

Ingredients

Strawberry, blueberry, and raspberry-filled 1 cup of mixed berries

almond milk, 1 cup

a tbsp of chia seeds

1 teaspoon of honey

Preparation

In a blender, combine all the Ingredients.

Blend everything thoroughly until it's smooth.

To serve, pour into a glass.

44. Smoothie with pineapple, mint, and lime

Ingredients

1 cup of chunky pineapple

a few leaves of fresh mint

spinach leaves, 1 cup

Coconut water, 1 cup

1 teaspoon of honey

Preparation

To a blender, add all the Ingredients.

Blend till creamy and smooth.

Enjoy this smoothie to keep you cool!

45. Smoothie with Peach, Ginger, and Turmeric

Ingredients

Frozen peaches, 1 cup

fresh ginger root, peeled, 1/2 inch

fresh turmeric root, peeled, 1/2 inch

almond milk, 1 cup

1 teaspoon of honey

Preparation

Blend the items together in a blender.

Blend everything thoroughly until it's smooth.

To serve, pour into a glass.

CONCLUSION

Smoothies have become an effective tool in the treatment of arthritis. The fusion of nutrient-rich components, anti-inflammatory qualities, and focused feeding has the potential to improve overall joint health while reducing symptoms and pain.

We have observed the life-changing effects that these vivid elixirs can have on people as we have explored and developed smoothie recipes that are especially suited for arthritis. Numerous people have reported finding relief from arthritis symptoms by incorporating smoothies into their daily routines, which is a testimonial to the effectiveness of this strategy.

Smoothies provide a tasty and practical approach to provide the body the vitamins, minerals, antioxidants, and anti-inflammatory substances it needs. We can give our joints the support they require to thrive and perform at their best by utilizing the power of nature.

It is important to keep in mind that each person's experience is different as you travel along the road to arthritis treatment. It's crucial to pay attention to your body, seek the advice of medical professionals, and personalize your smoothie selections to meet your unique requirements and preferences.

With the information and recipes included in this smoothie recipe book, you are now equipped to set out on your own path to managing your arthritis and enhancing your quality of life. The smoothie recipes provided here offer a variety of options to meet your interests and goals, whether you're wanting to decrease inflammation, improve joint health, or simply enjoy a pleasant and healthy beverage.

So raise a glass to a life free from arthritis' grip and one that is vibrant and healthy. Discover the delight of nourishing your body from the inside out by embracing the power of smoothies as a crucial element of your arthritis management strategy. Cheers to greater vitality, mobility, and wellbeing in the future!

Printed in Great Britain
by Amazon